Brought by Mr. Thos. Major Engraver Two Copper Plates for the One Penny Duty on N
the One Numberd from 151 to 175 the other from 176 to 200 Inclusive & the Impressions whereof are
Numberd, In Witness whereof We have hereunto set our Hands the 10th May 1765 By Order of the

We do hereby Acknowledge to have this Day Received back the Above mentioned Copp
among the other Plates & Dies used in the Service of the Stamp Revenue, to be kept accordin
of the Office, Witness our Hands the 10th May 1765

THE BRITISH LIBRARY

TREASURES IN FOCUS

Stamps

THE BRITISH LIBRARY HAS ONE of the greatest philatelic collections in the world, featuring many rare and attractive stamps. Developed from a number of bequests and donations, including that of the great collector Thomas Tapling, it is a "living treasure" of stamps, postal stationery, philatelic objects and machinery that grows in size every year. A large part of the collection is on public exhibition. This book is designed to add some detail to the stories of these small pieces of paper which are familiar to anyone who has posted or received a letter, and whose eye has been caught by the small splash of colour in the corner of the envelope.

Most people would correctly guess that the British Library's smallest objects are to be found in its Philatelic Collections, but perhaps not its largest and heaviest object too! The latter is the only surviving Perkins D cylinder printing press which dates from 1819 and from 1840 would have been used by the printer, Perkins, Bacon & Petch, to produce the one (1d) penny black and two (2d) pence blue. Subsequently it printed most of the early stamps of the British Empire. The press is briefly described and is illustrated on page 9.

The first postage stamps to be introduced in May 1840 were the penny (1d) black and two pence (2d) blue. The image that formed the basis of this famous stamp was of Queen Victoria's head in profile by William Wyon, and was taken from a medal commemorating her visit to the Corporation of London in 1837. While many countries had yet to introduce a uniform charge, they did adopt the postage stamp, with the cantons of Zurich and of Geneva, and Brazil in 1843, Basle in 1845, United States and Mauritius in 1847, Bermuda in 1848, France, Belgium and Bavaria in 1849. By 1870 most of the major, and a few minor, countries had stamps.

The introduction of uniform 1d postage in Great Britain and Ireland in January 1840 marked the end of a campaign by the pressure group Mercantile Committee on Postage, and the Parliamentary Select Committee on Postage. Those involved in the cause for postal reform included Robert Wallace MP,

Rowland Hill and Henry Cole. Before 1840 letters were charged by distance and the number of sheets of paper they comprised, with the receiver of the letter, not the sender paying the postage! In addition another penny was added if the letter crossed the Menai Bridge in Wales and ½d if conveyed in Scotland by a mail carriage with more than two wheels! A two page letter travelling between 80 and 120 miles was charged one shilling and sixpence (1/6d) but from 10th January 1840 the charge was just 1d if under half an ounce in weight. These changes transformed the ease, expense and speed of sending correspondence, especially with the development of railways in the mid-nineteenth century.

The stamp to pay postage is better known to the world than the tax, revenue or fiscal stamp. The first of these revenue or non-postage stamps was introduced in Holland in 1624 to help pay for their war with Spain for independence. It took the form of an impressed seal stamped on paper for legal documents which formed a tax on the transaction. In Great Britain similar impressed or embossed stamps were introduced in 1694, the same year as the Bank of England was formed, and for the same purpose of raising money, in this case, to fight the French. These stamps took the form of colourless embossing for legal documents and ranged in face value from 1d to 40/-. The Stamp Office (now part of HM Revenue and Customs) was established at the same time to administer the collecting of these taxes, and was later to be responsible, under direction from Rowland Hill working in the Treasury, for the production of the 1840 postage stamps. This same office still embosses red revenue stamps on property deeds today.

Perhaps the most significant printed tax stamps were those introduced in 1765 to raise money to defend the American Colonies against any aggression by the French. So unpopular was the tax that rioting took place in Boston and the slogan 'no taxation without representation' was coined. This was an early sign of the tension between British and American Colonies which resulted in the War of Independence and the formation of the United States of America in 1775. A proof sheet of these rare stamps is shown on page 10.

THE TAPLING COLLECTION

The Tapling Collection is without doubt the British Library's best known and most important philatelic collection. It is unique in that it is the only major philatelic collection formed in the nineteenth century which remains intact today. Its owner, the industrialist and MP Thomas Tapling (1855-91), had sufficient wealth to purchase some of the most important postage stamps, postal stationery and collections of his day, many of which are included in this book.

Following the formation of the Philatelic Society, London (now The Royal Philatelic Society London) in 1869, Tapling became a member in about 1871 and was elected to the Committee in 1876. He became Vice-President in 1881 at the age of twenty six and would undoubtedly have become President had he not died from tuberculosis at the age of thirty five.

While Tapling purchased many single items he was able, because of his wealth, to acquire complete postage stamp collections. Without doubt the most significant collection to be purchased was that formed by the French brothers Gustave (1848-94) and Martial (1853-1910) Caillebotte. Gustave was one of the lesser-known impressionist painters of the period. When Martial married in 1887 the brothers decided to sell their collection. A significant part of this large holding was sold to Tapling for a sum said to be £5,000 (today - based on average earnings - this would be over £2.5 million) and it is estimated that this doubled the size of his collection.

When Thomas Tapling died in 1891 he bequeathed his collection of postage stamps and postal stationery to the Trustees of the British Museum. It was rearranged by the collection's first Curator Edward (later Sir Edward) Denny Bacon (1860-1938). So large was the task that it took him and his assistant Miss Jane Hamilton (1874-1957) from 1892 to 1899 to complete. From 1903 much of the Tapling Collection has been on public exhibition. When the British Library was formed in 1973 it was transferred to that organisation, and now forms a significant part of the Library's collection of stamps and philatelic material.

OPPOSITE The press, correctly a "Perkins D cylinder", was developed for intaglio printing (also known as recess or line-engraved) by Jacob Perkins and patented in 1819. It was one of several used to print the 1d black (the Penny Black) and 2d blue: the first postage stamps of Great Britain and Ireland, which were issued in 1840. The Stamp Office of the Inland Revenue ordered them from the printers Perkins, Bacon & Petch for the General Post Office. The press was also used for printing many of the early stamps for British Colonial territories ordered by the Crown Agents from 1853. These include stamps for Cape of Good Hope, Ceylon, Mauritius, St Helena, Trinidad, and Western Australia; and by direct contract for the Ionian Islands, New Brunswick, New South Wales, New Zealand, and Victoria.

RIGHT Great Britain: 1840 1d black, the first postage stamp.

LEFT AND BELOW America: Revenue 1765 Newspaper and Pamphlet One Penny. A proof sheet of 26 impressions, showing the registration certificate. (The Board of Inland Revenue Stamping Department Archive)

These tax stamps were issued as a result of the Stamp Act of 1765 to contribute towards the costs of defending the American Colonies from the French. The tax was mainly imposed on legal documents, licenses, newspapers, pamphlets and almanacs in the thirteen American Colonies plus Quebec, Nova Scotia, Newfoundland, Florida, the Bahamas and the West Indian Islands. Opposition was swift, protest meetings were held, major rioting took place and the cry of 'no taxation without representation' was made. So unpopular was the tax that it was abandoned some months later, but relations with the American Colonies had been greatly damaged and this contributed to the background of the War of Independence in 1775.

LEFT Barbados: 1861-70 1/- blue error of colour, unused. (The Tapling Collection)

The first consignment of the 1/- stamp of the 1861-70 series, showing Britannia, were sent out to Barbados by the printers, Perkins, Bacon & Company of London in April, 1863. The 50,000 stamps should have been printed in brown-black, but on arrival they were found to have been erroneously printed in blue, the colour of the 1d stamp. Almost all of the errors were returned to England, to be exchanged for new stock in the correct colour. A few examples were kept for a "*postage label album*". Less than a dozen are known to exist today.

BELOW British Guiana: 1850-51 4 cents lemon-yellow, cut square used on entire. (The Tapling Collection)

This was one of the first issues of postage stamps made for British Guiana, now Guyana. They were printed from newspaper type in the office of the Royal Gazette, Georgetown. As a security measure they were initialed by the postal officials before issue. Scissors rather than perforations were used to separate copies and this is one of two letters known with this stamp affixed and cut square rather than cut round.

ABOVE AND OPPOSITE Bulgaria: 1882 5 stotinki rose and pale rose, error of colour, used on entire with 10 stotinki. (The Tapling Collection)

These early stamps of Bulgaria show the Lion of Bulgaria Coat of Arms, and were printed by the [Russian] State Printing Works in St. Petersburg. In the third issue of this design made in 1882, a sheet of the 5 stotinki was printed in error in the colours of the 10 stotinki rose and pale rose, rather than the correct green and pale green. The 5 stotinki error is shown here, used on an envelope together with a 10 stotinki. Few of these errors are known to have survived.

G. ZARMIKIAN, SOFIA.

Principauté de Bulgarie

R

No

1049

Monsieur

Arthur Maury

8 Cité Malesherbes

Paris

France

BELOW **Canada: 1851 12d black an unused horizontal pair from the foot of the sheet. (The Tapling Collection)**

The first issue of stamps for the colony of Canada was made in 1851. 1/- was not used as the face value as the value of a shilling varied according to location. In New England 1/- meant sixteen and two-thirds cents which was equal to 10d. In New York a shilling meant twelve and a half cents equaling 7½d. In contrast, the face value of 12d was clear. Out of the 51,000 of the 12d black that were printed about 130 copies are believed to exist today and only five unused pairs.

BELOW **Canada: 1927 London to London flight semi official 25 cents dull green and yellow. (The Fitz Gerald Collection)**

These were prepared for an abortive attempt to fly across the Atlantic. Only one hundred of the stamps were printed, most of which were used on mail, which was lost when the plane disappeared into fog and was never heard of again. There are only ten copies known to exist today.

OPPOSITE **Cape of Good Hope: 1861 4d vermillion error of colour, in pair with 1d vermillion, used. (The Tapling Collection)**

The first stamps of the Cape of Good Hope were the famous triangular issue which first appeared in 1853. These were printed by two companies in London, but in addition a local provisional issue was made in Cape Town in 1861 to cope with a temporary shortage. This local issue had a 1d in red and a 4d in blue. The printing plates were made up of a number of individual clichés or printing blocks, however one cliché from each value was put into the wrong printing plate. This resulted in examples of both the 1d and 4d being printed in the wrong colour. The 4d error is shown here, in a pair with a normal 1d, such pairs are rare.

POSTAGE
FOUR PENCE
CAPE OF GOOD HOPE
CAPE OF GOOD HOPE
POSTAGE
ONE PENNY

OPPOSITE France: 1853-61 1 franc carmine, an unused tête-bêche pair. (The Tapling Collection)

Louis Napoleon became Emperor Napoleon III in 1852 and his head appears on the stamps of the 1853-61 series. Many of the early stamps of France exist where one of the impressions is upside-down in relation to those next to it, or tête-bêche. These tête-bêche varieties are something of a mystery as it is not known why the plate maker and printer, Anatole A Hulot, produced them in this way. This 1 franc carmine tête-bêche pair is one of the great rarities of French philately.

1 · F · POSTES · 1 · F
EMPIRE · FRANC

EMPIRE · FRANC
1 · F · POSTES · 1 · F

Stronger blue-bla colour.

RIGHT Germany: 1947-48 2 pfennig brown-black, 16 pfennig blue-green, 25 pfennig orange, 60 pfennig red, 80 pfennig grey-blue and 84 pfennig green, colour trials on card. (The Foreign Office Collection)

After the defeat of Germany following the 1939-45 war, the country was divided into four Zones of Occupation. All designs and colours for postage stamps were subject to approval by the four occupying military powers (American, British, French and Soviet). The signatures of army officers from the four powers indicated such approval. Some of the stamps shown are in colours or designs which were not issued.

(For revised colours see card D.)

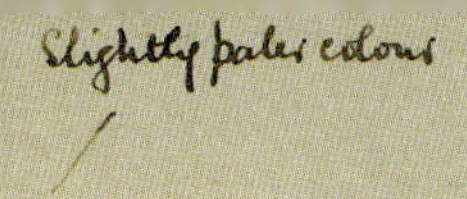

Lighter & brighter green

[illegible] CCCP.

[illegible]

[illegible] (Br.)

[illegible] (U.S.A.)

OPPOSITE Gold Coast: 1883 1d on 4d magenta, used. (The Tapling Collection)

The supply of 1d stamps in Gold Coast had become short in 1883 and a way had to be found to account for the money taken. In some cases 2d stamps were cut in half or "bisected", each half being used for 1d. In the case of the stamp illustrated, a "1d" surcharge was applied to a 4d stamp, turning it into a 1d stamp. Only one copy of this surcharged stamp has been recorded.

POSTAGE
GOLD
COAST
FOUR PENCE

ABOVE Great Britain: 1858-79 1d red Plate 77, unused. (The Tapling Collection)

In 1858 it was decided to number the printing plates used for British postage stamps. The first issued stamp to be so numbered was plate 71 and the last of this series was plate 225, which was issued in 1879. Some plates were found to be defective and not used and this was the case with plate 77. This unused copy is one of only nine recorded. The plate number is to be found printed twice on each stamp in the side panels.

BELOW **Great Britain: 1857 envelope bearing 1856-58 1d red used within London, with "NORTHERN DISTRICT/N" postcode label attached. (The Fletcher Collection)**

District Sorting Offices in London were established in 1856, with ten offices covering the postcode districts WC, EC, N, NE, E, SE, S, SW, W and NW. To help promote the new scheme small labels were produced to be affixed to envelopes. This is one of only a handful of envelopes bearing these labels known to exist.

BELOW Great Britain: 1913 King George V Seahorse master die proof in sepia. (The Harrison Collection)

The attractive high value stamps, 2/6, 5/-, 10/- and £1 of the Seahorses design, were first issued in 1913. The engraver, J A C Harrison, prepared a die which had a single image of the design. This die was then used to prepare the printing plates, which had eighty images upon it. As the engraver proceeded with his work on the die, he took proofs to check his progress. A progressive proof of the master die in sepia is shown here.

ABOVE Great Britain: 1918-19 Seahorse Bradbury, Wilkinson 2/6, a printer's proof sheet of eighty in blue, each overprinted "SPECIMEN". (The Board of Inland Revenue Stamping Department Archive)

The Seahorse stamps were printed in sheets of eighty, which were cut into two and supplied to post offices in sheets of forty. Shown here is part of a printer's proof sheet of the 2/6 value in blue (the colour of the 10/-), instead of the issued colour of sepia or brown. This is a colour trial which has been overprinted "SPECIMEN".

BELOW Great Britain: Telegraphs: 1876-81 £5 essay. (The Langmead Collection)

Large areas of the British Isles were without telegraph services in the 1860s. This led to a demand for the private telegraph companies to be nationalised and the telegraph network was taken over by the Post Office in 1870. Special stamps were used to pay for telegraph services in a similar way to postage stamps. Shown is the unique original artwork, or essay, for the £5 stamp. It was issued in 1877 in orange, and in 1882 was issued as a postage stamp after the substitution of the word "POSTAGE" for the word "TELEGRAPHS" in the design.

ABOVE Hawaii: 1851-52 2 cents blue, type 1, used. (The Tapling Collection)

Before the annexation of Hawaii by the United States in 1898, the country had been independent, and until 1893 a monarchy. American Missionaries had settled in the islands from 1820 and much of the mail was to and from the United States. A postal service was established in 1850; stamps were first issued in 1851 and printed at the Government Printing Office, Honolulu. At first these stamps only covered local postage (inscribed "Hawaiian Postage") but from 1852 covered local and United States postage (inscribed "H.I. & U.S. Postage"). The "Missionary issue", as these are known, are amongst the rarest stamps, and only seventeen of the 2 cents exist.

OPPOSITE India: 1854 4 annas blue and pale red, error head inverted, two used on cover. (The Tapling Collection)

The first general issue of stamps for British India appeared in 1854. These were half anna blue, 1 anna red, 2 anna green and 4 annas blue and red, printed from lithographic stones at the office of the Surveyor-General, in Calcutta. As the 4 annas was in two colours it required two printings from separate lithographic stones, one for the head of Queen Victoria in blue, and one for the frame in red. The two copies of the 4 annas shown on this letter sheet from Bombay to Venice, have the head of Queen Victoria printed upside down. This is the only known entire bearing the error image of the head inverted (the stamps are affixed upside down). Thomas Tapling purchased the item for £32 in 1890 from the Italian stamp dealer Dr Emilio Diena

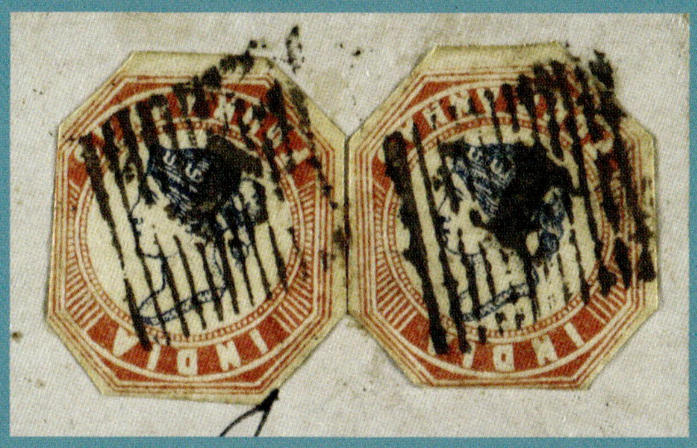

BELOW AND OPPOSITE Jamaica: 1860-70 1/- in a black proof sheet (detail). (The Board of Inland Revenue Stamping Department Archive)

Postage stamps for Jamaica were first issued in 1860. They were printed in London by Thomas De La Rue and the values were 1d, 2d, 3d, 4d, 6d and 1/-. Shown is a plate proof in black of the 1/- value. The second stamp from the left in the second row shows a small flaw in the printing plate, this is known as the "dollar variety". The S in Shilling is malformed as a $ and can clearly be seen in this proof which is unique.

173

STAMPS, £3.

JAMAICA
£1
TOBACCO GROWING & CIGAR MAKING

OPPOSITE **Jamaica: 1956-58 £1 chocolate and violet, unissued.** (The Crown Agents Collection)

The £1 stamp issued in the reign of King George VI shows tobacco growing and cigar making. The first £1 stamp for Queen Elizabeth II was to have been in the same design and colours, but this was abandoned after they had been printed. Shown here is the unissued stamp showing the portrait of the Queen, of which only seven examples exist.

OPPOSITE AND ABOVE **Mauritius: 1847, "Post Office" 1d orange-red used on cover, and 2d deep blue, unused. (The Tapling Collection)**

The first British Colonial postage stamps were issued in Mauritius in 1847. These are the famous “Post Office” issue, so called because of the inscription in the left margin. The design and colours were based upon the then current stamps of Great Britain. Some of the 1d

stamps were used on covers that contained invitations to a ball organised by Lady Gomm, the wife of the Governor. Three such covers exist today. The 2d blue is known as the *Blue Mauritius*, and altogether only fourteen copies of the 1d orange-red and twelve copies of the 2d deep blue are known to exist. These stamps are considered as some of the most famous and important of all the philatelic rarities.

BELOW **New South Wales: 1850 1d and 3d essays of the Sydney View issue. (The Tapling Collection)**

The first stamps of New South Wales, were issued in 1850. The design is a view of Sydney with a seated figure releasing convicts from their shackles, and the motto *Sic fortis Etruria crevit* (Thus mighty Etruria grew) is a quotation from Virgil. They are known to collectors as "Sydney Views". Shown are the unique original essays or artwork for the 1d and 3d stamps. The space between the essays was originally occupied by a 2d essay, which is now in the Royal Philatelic Collection.

ABOVE **New Zealand: 1857 1d dull orange, "Dwarf", used. (The Tapling Collection)**

The early stamps of New Zealand were printed on similar printing presses to the Penny Black, (see page 8). The initial printing of 1855 was produced in London, but, the printing plates and a press were later sent to New Zealand. This locally printed 1d stamp shows a remarkable error, being overlapped double printed. It is thought that half way through the printing of the stamp the press malfunctioned, because the impressions were not accurately aligned. This stamp has a short appearance, and so is known to philatelists as the "Dwarf". Only two examples are recorded.

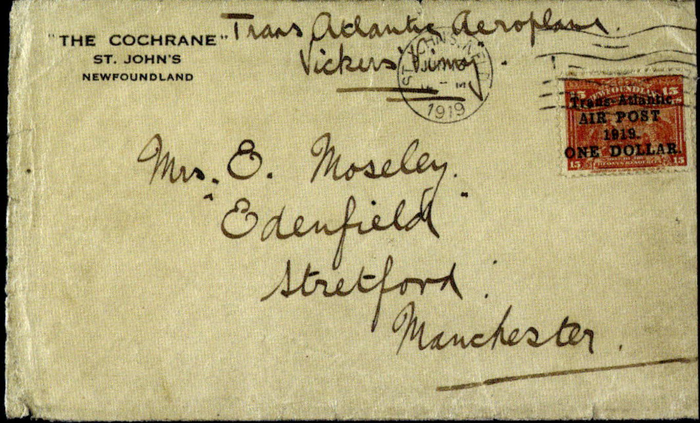

ABOVE Newfoundland: 1919 cover carried on Alcock and Brown's first Trans-Atlantic flight, (addressed to Alcock's sister), bearing 1919 (9 June) $1 on 15 cents bright scarlet. (The Fitz Gerald Collection)

The first successful non-stop crossing of the Atlantic was made by Alcock and Brown, leaving from Newfoundland on 14th June 1919. Shown here is an envelope carried on the flight and addressed to Mrs E Moseley, Alcock's sister in Manchester. The message enclosed read "...This letter will travel with me in the official mail bag, the first to be carried over the Atlantic..."

BELOW Northern Nigeria: 1904 £25 green and carmine. (The Mosely Collection)

This stamp, although inscribed "Postage & Revenue" was used only for tax or revenue purposes and in particular a fee for liquor licenses. Twenty-five pounds in 1904 was a considerable sum of money. The Northern Nigerian authorities requested only 120 stamps which would have been just one sheet. Eventually 1,080 stamps were printed in nine sheets of 120 stamps per sheet at a cost of 16/8. None of these stamps were overprinted "Specimen" for the purpose of distribution as examples to member post offices of the Universal Postal Union. This reinforces the fact that these are revenue and not postage stamps.

LEFT **Orange Free State: 1878 5/-, the die. (The General Collection)**

The first series of postage stamps for the Orange Free State were issued between 1868 and 1878. Thomas De La Rue & Co of London was asked to produce the stamps. De La Rue made a master die, which was then used to make an individual die for each of the values in the series. These dies were used to make the printing plates, each of which would print 240 stamps. Shown is the 5/- die together with the stamp as issued.

ABOVE Rumania, Moldavia: 1858 81 parale blue on blue paper, unused. (The Tapling Collection)

The first postage stamps issued in 1858 for Rumania (now Romania) were those for Moldavia, then an independent principality. These are the rare and famous "Bulls", based on Moldavia's emblem, a bull's head. The stamps were for 27, 54, 81 and 108 parale and only 684 are recorded still to exist. The rarest is the 81 parale with just sixty-two still existing. In 1861 Moldavia joined with Wallachia to form Rumania.

OPPOSITE St Helena: 1961 Tristan Relief Fund 5c+6d, 7½c+9d, and 10c+1/-, used on a postcard. (The Foreign and Commonwealth Office Collection)

The small island of Tristan da Cunha in the South Atlantic hit the headlines in October 1961 when violent volcanic activity caused the evacuation of the population. The authorities on the neighbouring island of St. Helena, some 1,400 miles to the north-east, started a Relief Fund, and a supply of Tristan da Cunha stamps were surcharged "ST. HELENA Tristan Relief" with an amount for the fund. Shown is the postcard, bearing three of the four values in the set, sent by the Governor of St Helena to "The Rt. Hon. Reginald Maudling, MP, Secretary of State for the Colonies" informing him of the new stamps. Unfortunately only the Colonial Office in London could authorise new stamps, a fact clearly unknown to the Governor, and so the issue was withdrawn. These are among the rarest of modern stamps as only 434 sets were sold.

Albatross chick on nest
at Nightingale Island.

Sold in aid of
the St. Helena Fund for Tristan.

The Castle,
St. Helena.
12 October 1961

(Unnumbered).

Sir,

I have the honour to transmit some postage stamps about which I will write at greater length when I have more space at my command.

I have the honour to be,
Sir,
Your most obedient, humble servant,

Robert Alford

Governor.

The Rt. Hon. Reginald Maudling, M.P.
Secretary of State for the Colonies.
Colonial Office.
Church House.
Great Smith Street.
London SW1.

ABOVE Spain: 1851 2 reales blue, error of colour. (The Tapling Collection)

The second issue of postage stamps for Spain appeared in 1851, with six values of similar design, including the 2 reales in red, and 6 reales in blue. The 2 reales error of colour was caused by the accidental insertion of a 2 reales cliché in the printing plate of the 6 reales. This was then printed in blue, giving the error. Only three copies of the stamp are recorded to have survived and this one was the first to be found. It was subjected to a test for authenticity sometimes made in the nineteenth century – it was boiled! This treatment removed almost all of the postmark of which only a smudge remains today.

BELOW **Swaziland: Revenue 1956 £5 black and red, unused. (The Foreign and Commonwealth Office Collection)**

Revenue or tax stamps were issued in Swaziland from 1890. In 1956 a £5 value was required and was printed in the design first used for postage and revenue purposes in 1938. Just 12,000 examples of the £5 stamp were printed but a small number, perhaps as low as ten, have survived. In 1961 with the adoption of the rand the stock was overprinted R10.

RIGHT Sweden: 1872-79 20 öre vermilion, a used vertical pair on piece, lower stamp error TRETIO. (The Tapling Collection)

A new series of postage stamps was issued in 1872 with values from 3 öre to 1 riksdaler. The stamps were reprinted as required including the 20 öre vermilion. In preparing for a new printing in 1879 it was noticed that one of the printing clichés was damaged. To save on time and expense a 30 öre cliché with the number 30 and the words TRETIO was inserted into the plate in the place of the defective one. Both number and words were to be removed, but in error only the number 30 was removed with the words TRETIO remaining, resulting in one error per sheet of 100. Something over fifty copies of the error still exist.

BELOW Switzerland: Zurich 1843 4 rappen, an unused horizontal strip of five. (The Tapling Collection)

In 1843, Switzerland was the second country after Great Britain to issue postage stamps, when the canton of Zurich issued 4 and 6 rappen values. Unlike the British 1d black and 2d blue, the main feature of the design is the face value. These were printed by lithography by Orell, Fussli & Company of Zurich. In 1850 the stamps of Federal Switzerland superseded them. The 4 rappen horizontal strip of five is the largest known unsevered multiple and thus unique.

BELOW **Transvaal: 1870 imperforate 1/- deep green, an unused tête-bêche pair. (The Tapling Collection)**

Transvaal, formerly South African Republic, and now part of South Africa, issued stamps from 1870. The printing plates were first made and used by Adolph Otto of Gustrow, Mecklenburg-Schwerin, in Germany. Until 1883 these and other similar printing plates were

used by a variety of local printers in Transvaal, including using them subsequently overprinted during the first British occupation following annexation in 1876. The 6d and 1/- plates are known with one of the impressions upside-down in relation to those next to it or tête-bêche. This is the only recorded tête-bêche pair of the 1/- deep green of 1870.

VAN DIEMENS LAND
POSTAGE
ONE PENNY

VAN DIEMENS LAND
POSTAGE
TWO PENCE

VAN DIEMENS LAND
POSTAGE
FOUR PENCE

TASMANIA
SIX PENCE

OPPOSITE **Tasmania/Van Diemens Land: 1855-71 Chalon Head design, 1d, 2d, 4d, and 6d die proofs in colour. (The Supplementary Collection)**

The Supplementary Collection includes a wonderful group of coloured die proofs printed by Thomas De La Rue & Company from plates made by Perkins, Bacon & Company after the latter lost the Colonial printing contract in 1862. These die proofs were produced for exhibition and were donated by the Crown Agents in 1900.

ABOVE **United States: Carrier's stamps, Charleston, Honour's City Post 1849 2 cents black on entire with General issue 1847 5 cents, a horizontal pair. (The Tapling Collection)**

In the 1840s the Government postal service in the United States carried mail only from town to town and with no local delivery to a house or business. If mail was to be delivered it could be consigned to a private local post. The cover shown was sent from Charleston to Washington DC, with local delivery by Honour's City Post.

LEFT United States: Confederate States 1862 5 cents, the die. (The General Collection)

During the American Civil War of 1861-5 the Confederate States of America issued its own stamps. In 1862 a supply of 5 cents blue together with the printing plate was ordered from Thomas De La Rue & Company of London. The first printing was made in London, and afterwards from the same plate by Archer & Daly of Richmond, Virginia. Shown is the original die from which the plate was made.

ABOVE United States: 1869 15 cents blue and brown, error centre inverted, used. (The Tapling Collection)

The 1869 issue of postage stamps for the United States comprised values from 1 cent to 90 cents. The 15 to 90 cents values are printed in two colours, requiring two passes through the press. Copies of the 15 cents (showing the landing of Columbus), 24 cents (showing the Declaration of Independence) and 30 cents (showing flags) were printed in error with one of the colours upside down or inverted. These are some of the rarest stamps from the United States.

BELOW United States: 1918 Airmail 24 cents blue and carmine, error centre Curtiss Jenny aircraft inverted. (The Fitz Gerald Collection)

In 1918 the United States issued a set of stamps for use on air mail letters. These were in 6, 16 and 24 cents values. The 24 cents stamp was printed in blue and carmine which required printings from two separate plates, one for each colour. In error, the blue colour of the aircraft was printed upside down, creating one of the world's best known stamps. A sheet of 100 stamps was purchased by a philatelist in 1918, and only that number still exist.

BELOW United States: Postmasters Provisional St Louis 1845-6 10 cents, used. (The Tapling Collection)

Before the first issue of postage stamps was ready for use in all parts of the United States in 1847, local postmasters made provisional issues. The provisional stamps for St Louis, Missouri were 5 and 10 cents values, showing the Missouri Coat of Arms and were designed and printed by J M Kershaw. Printing was from a copper plate with three 5 cents and three 10 cents in a sheet of six and 500 were so produced. It was later altered to include 20 cents values.

RIGHT Uruguay: 1858 120 centavos blue, an unused tête-bêche pair. (The Tapling Collection)

The second issue of postage stamps for Uruguay appeared in 1858 in 120, 180, and 240 centavos values. These are inscribed "Montevideo" and were printed in sheets of seventy-eight or two hundred and four (240 centavos). One of the impressions for the 120 and 180 centavos was inverted, and this has resulted in some of the world's rarest stamps when in pairs one is inverted in relation to the other or tête-bêche. Of the 120 centavos only three and of the 180 centavos only two tête-bêche pairs exist.

ABOVE Western Australia: 1854-55 4d blue, error frame inverted, used. (The Tapling Collection)

The first Western Australian stamp, a 1d black, was issued in 1854 and was printed by Perkins, Bacon in London. The need for 4d and 1/- stamps was soon established and these were printed in Western Australia from lithographic printing stones with transfers derived from the 1d stamps. The 4d and 1/- stamps were made up of two transfers, one for the image of the Swan and one for the frame or lettering. In placing one of the transfers for the frame for the 4d value it became upside-down or inverted in relation to the Swan. The resulting stamps, error "frame inverted", are some of the rarest, only fourteen being recorded. For many years it was believed that the error was "inverted swan" until the original printing stone was found, and the truth discovered.

BELOW Western Australia: 1864-79 2d mauve, error of colour, unused. (The Tapling Collection)

The 1864-79 series of postage stamps for Western Australia were printed in London by Thomas De La Rue. The 2d value should have been yellow in colour, but in error some were printed in mauve (the colour of the 6d value) and issued in 1879. The printers did not realise the mistake and the stamps were printed and sold as 6d values. This makes them technically speaking an error of value rather than of colour.

The British Library would like to thank the following for their help in producing *Treasures in Focus: Stamps*: David Beech, Paul Skinner, Bobby Birchall and Catherine Britton.

Glossary
1d: one penny
2d: two pence
/- a shilling (twelve pence)
Colour trial: A printed proof in colour or colours made to select the colour or colours in which a stamp should be printed
Die: a metal device from which the printing plate is cut or moulded
Entire: a folded letter sheet
Essay: a suggested or proposed design for a stamp
Imperforate: without perforations
Tête-bêche: one stamp inverted or upside-down in relation to the adjacent stamp.

All images are taken from the Philatelic Collections of the British Library.

First published 2009 by
The British Library
96 Euston Road
London
NW1 2DB

British Library Cataloguing in Publication Data
A catalogue record for this book is available from
The British Library

ISBN 978-0-7123-0953-0

Designed and typeset by Bobby & Co, London
Colour reproductions by Dot Gradations Ltd, UK
Printed and bound in Italy by Printer Trento S.r.l.